Can You Find It?

Identify and Describe Shapes

Christine Shumer

ROSEN
COMMON CORE MATH
READERS

Rosen Classroom™

I0792496

New York

Published in 2014 by The Rosen Publishing Group, Inc.
29 East 21st Street, New York, NY 10010

Book Design: Mickey Harmon

Photo Credits: Cover Lifesize/Thinkstock.com; p. 5 art&design/Shutterstock.com; p. 7 (tree) F1online/Thinkstock.com; pp. 7 (kite), 9 (classroom) iStockphoto/Thinkstock.com; p. 9 (clock) Ryan McVay/Thinkstock.com; p. 11 (trees) defpicture /Shutterstock.com; p. 11 Svetlana Larina/Shutterstock.com; p. 13 (landscape) Galyna Andrushko/Shutterstock.com; p. 13 (light) krsmanovic/Shutterstock.com; p. 15 Ekaterina Pokrovsky/Shutterstock.com.

ISBN: 978-1-4777-1647-2
6-pack ISBN: 978-1-4777-1648-9

Manufactured in the United States of America

CPSIA Compliance Information: Batch #CS13RC: For further information contact Rosen Publishing, New York, New York at 1-800-237-9932.

Word Count: 102

Contents

Shapes are everywhere!
If you look closely, they're easy to see.

Can you find a diamond?
The kite is a diamond.
The kite in the sky is
near a tree.

Can you find a circle?
The clock at my school
is a circle.
The clock is above the door.

Can you find the rectangle?
The frame is a rectangle.
The frame is beside the bed.

Can you find a square?
The picture on the wall
is a square.
The picture is below the light.

Can you find a triangle?
The sign is a triangle.
The sign is in front of the car.

Words to Know

diamond

frame

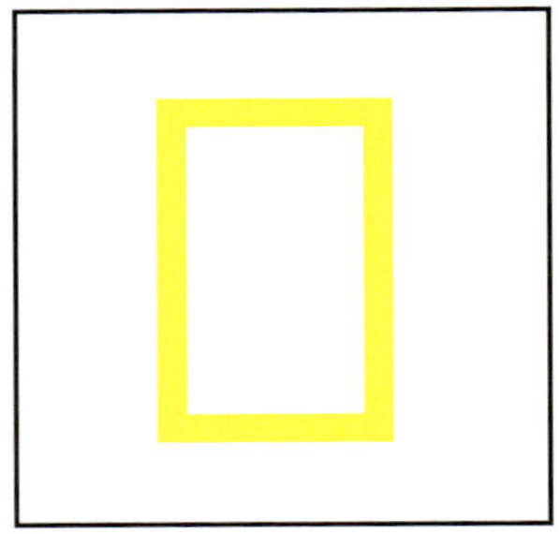
rectangle

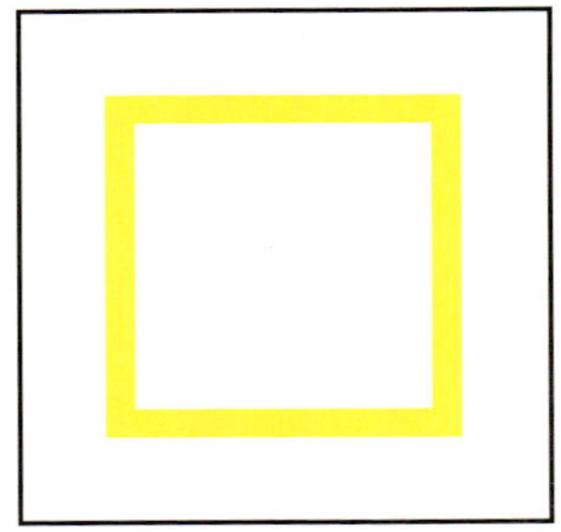
square

Index